Army Cats

Books by Tom Sleigh

Poetry

Army Cats
Space Walk
Bula Matari/Smasher of Rocks (Limited Edition)
Far Side of the Earth
The Dreamhouse
The Chain
Waking
After One

Essays

Interview with a Ghost

Translation

Herakles by Euripides

Army Cats

Poems

Tom Sleigh

Graywolf Press

This publication is made possible by funding provided in part by a
grant from the Minnesota State Arts Board, through an appropriation by the
Minnesota State Legislature, a grant from the National Endowment for the Arts, and
private funders. Significant support has also been provided by Target; the McKnight
Foundation; and other generous contributions from foundations, corporations, and
individuals. To these organizations and individuals we offer our heartfelt thanks.

Published by Graywolf Press
250 Third Avenue North, Suite 600
Minneapolis, Minnesota 55401

www.graywolfpress.org

Published in the United States of America

ISBN 978-1-55597-583-8

2 4 6 8 9 7 5 3 1
First Graywolf Printing, 2011

Library of Congress Control Number: 2011920673

Cover design: Kyle G. Hunter

Cover photo: Yasuhide Fumoto, Getty Images

Contents

ONE

Army Cats   5

Beirut Tank   8

Border Crossings   10

Stranding   12

Refugee   15

For the Executive Director of the Fallen   16

Revenant   19

Pig from Ohio   22

A Wedding at Cana, Lebanon, 2007   24

Reporter   26

"This Thing of Darkness"   28

A Promise   32

Hunter Gatherer   33

After a Rembrandt Motif   36

The Games   37

Spell   41

TWO

To Death   45

The Chosen One   46

For a Spacesuit Set Adrift   48

O. D.   51

Money   54

Fenix   55

Round   59

-Triumph   60

THREE

Speech for a Fly   65

Through the Lens   66

A Woman at a Table   69

On First Avenue and Sixth Street   73

Self-Portrait with Shoulder Pads   78

For Benny Andrews   80

Orders of Daylight   82

Recording   87

Song That Can Only Be Sung Once   89

Mingus Reborn as Mingus   92

Army Cats

ONE

Army Cats

1

Over by the cemetery next to the CP
you could see them in wild catmint going crazy:
I watched them roll and wriggle, paw it, lick it,
chew it, leap about, pink tongues stuck out, drooling.

Cats in the tanks' squat shadows lounging.
Or sleeping curled up under gun turrets.
Hundreds of them sniffing or licking
long hind legs stuck into the air,

great six-toed brutes fixing you with a feral,
slit-eyed stare . . . everywhere ears twitching,
twitching as the armor plate expanding
in the heat gave off piercing little pings.

Cat invasion of the mind. Cat tribes
running wild. And one big pregnant
female comes racing through weeds to pounce
between the paws of a marble dog

crouching on a grave and sharpens
her claws against his beard of moss
before she goes all silky, luxuriously
squirming right under the dog's jaws,

and rolls over to expose her swollen belly.
Picture her with gold hoop earrings
and punked-out nose ring like the cat goddess Bast,
bronze kittens at her feet, the crowd drinking wildly,

women lifting up their skirts as she floats down
the Nile, a sistrum jangling in her paw.
Then come back out of it and sniff
her ointments, Lady of Flame, Eye of Ra.

2

Through the yard the tanks come gunning,
charioteers laughing, goggles smeared with dust
and sun, scattering the toms slinking
along the blast wall holding back the waves

from washing away white crosses on the graves,
the motors roaring through the afternoon
like a cat fuck yowling on and on.
The gun turrets revolving in the cats' eyes

swivel and shine, steel treads clanking,
sending the cats flying in an exodus
through brown brittle grass, the stalks
barely rippling as they pass.

3

After the last car bomb killed three soldiers
the army website labelled them "martyrs."
Four civilians killed at checkpoints. Three on the airport road.
A young woman blown up by a grenade.

Facts and more facts . . . until the dead ones
climb up out of the graves, gashes on faces
or faces blown away like sandblasted stone
that in the boarded up museum's

fractured English "leaves the onlooker
riddled and shaken, nothing but a pathetic gaping . . ."
And then I remember the ancient archers
frozen between reverence and necessity—

who stare down the enemy, barbarians,
as it's told, who nailed sacred cats to their shields,
knowing their foes outraged in their piety
would throw down their bows and wail like kittens.

Beirut Tank

Staring up into the tank's belly
lit by a bare bulb hanging down
off the exhaust, a mechanic's hands are up
inside the dark metallic innards doing something
that looks personal, private. This tank is nothing
like the ones the Americans deploy.
Those have uranium piercing shells that could melt
right through this tank's armor and set off
the ammo box: nothing can withstand the American tanks.

The barrel's called a cannon. The machine guns they call
deterrents. The tank is old, small, about the size
of a horse and cart. The armor plate shines green
under the streetlight. The sprockets, almost rusted out.
Somebody forgot to grease the nipples. The timing belt is nicked
and worn. The spare parts from France don't fit. This wire
crossed with this wire makes a catastrophic fire.
Be careful how you route it. .20 caliber ammo
goes in the hatch behind the armor plate.

The mechanic on his back in the dirt,
cursing in Arabic, sounds like he's cursing
in a good-natured way: who was the fucking moron
who did the maintenance on this thing?
This tank, this tank, he should push it off
a cliff into the sea to bob for
half an hour before sinking under the Pigeon Rocks
where all the lovers gather in the shadows
near that little bar, lit by a generator, that serves Arak

and warm beer to soldiers hanging out on the Corniche:
mainly conscripts from down south, whose orange groves
rot because nobody can pick the oranges: try to pick
an orange and a cluster bomb lodged in leaves
comes tumbling into your basket. What weight oil
did this cocksucker use, anyway? And this engine,
it's gonna blow. Beat up tanks and sandbags,
that's all this army is, old sparkplugs that get fouled
so that you have to file the gaps over and over.

He stares up in that live, minute, completely
concentrated way of scrutinizing something
or someone you thought you understood:
the tank's underbody completely covers his body,
they look like they're embracing when he reaches up
inside it, his needle nose pliers crimping, twisting,
pulling down hard. There, you see that, it's all corroded.
The cannon jutting out looks both threatening
and vulnerable as if the tank's firepower

were dependent on that wire. He runs two fingers
up and down it, then feels where rust,
mixed into an oily paste, shines like bloody flux
he gently dips his finger in, sniffs and tastes.
Clanging back his tapping on the armor plate,
as he listens to her talking on his back in the dirt, screwing in
the spare parts, the tank says what tanks always say,
Fix me, oil me, grease me, make it fit,
confirming what he knows about the French.

Border Crossings

1/ On the Train

Outback of the mind. Shiver of the fens
in oily desolation staining the swamp water
frozen over. Newark up ahead, the telephoto lens
of the heart homing in on a dead son or daughter.

If you wait long enough, the oil tanks and refineries
will stand up cleanly in the train windows
while light falling through itself falls through the gantries
trapping waste ground and weeds in cats-cradle shadows.

And in the ghost train the guy in uniform scared to be going
reminds me of you, pinned up on my wall,
Sgt. K. I. S. discharged Jan. 17 in Chaffee, Arkansas:

eyes averted from the stares of the living
who never called your name at roll call or mail call
and, failing to take your hand then, can't do so now.

2/ Trash Flowers

When you look at them, they look right back:
bareheaded survivors, one-eyed, soot-choked,
growing up out of rubble. The anti-garden where
whatever takes root just happens to find home

across the border from kids scrawling their names on bombs.
And among weeds camouflaging a fire-gutted tank,
a donkey, grazing, sniffs at the hot armor,
a stream of piss hissing past its flank . . .

Would my barking dogs of Brooklyn know their odor?
Piss on them too, just a drop for form's sake
and pass on? And the upstart narrator

gets out of the way of the olive trees
launching themselves root and branch into the sky
while oil tankers vaporize into ether.

3/ Ballad

When prayers were said, throats cut, the gods were thrown
in the ditch alongside the sacrifice.
But buoyed up out of blood by their boat of stone,
they sailed beyond the limits of this life.

And when I left the sandbagged museum
I thought of the mankilling time
of the fathers when True Thomas walked
past the end of night and could never come home

from Elfland if he spoke one word to the dark—
and before the garden green could he reach
and pull for his wages an apple from a tree

he waded through blood red to the knee,
for all the blood that's shed on earth
runs through the springs of that country.

Stranding

What came wafting
down the ditch
by the marsh grass waving
opened a hole
in the day through which,

like a puff of breath,
a ghost fountained up
rising in soft slo-mo,
lost, desolate, no place
left to go.

Dear bloody
Beirut and its internet cafés
were still smoking
from last night's
"little bombing."

Such threads, tattered sleeves
blown all over the street
from Emporio Armani.
Husband and wife shot
dead at the airport checkpoint.

Where else would this lead?
The investiture
of grieving takes all day
to sweep up in the tidal spillage
of plate glass.

What ish my nation,
asked Captain MacMorris
between battles.
But the ditch knows
just who we are—

and I see its only water
on a stealth raid
of the glimmer
hidden in the reeds.
And when I come close,

little scavenger flashings
and great claws held out rigidly
scuttle back into mud holes
drilling the bank.
Bending down to look,

I could smell the corruption's
gathering, sweetish odor,
its sonar gone haywire
driving it to shore.
What choices are you given,

what makes you want to swim
out of your own element?
The demure little ear-holes
and intelligent clear eyes,
the fate from birth sealed

inside its smile,
spent flukes and tail
being gnawed to bone.
The curt unrevealing stare
mirroring back my own.

Refugee

Her eyes alertly track my eyes staring
at her face so disfigured that I have to will
my eyes to keep on looking as she sits there
playing with her doll, telling it to mind her

mind her now, and then smiling at it
with what's left of her lips as if she were
the mother smiling at the child smiling
back at the mother: her face twisted up

by scars is a face of scars that's only hers,
her face that I look at as she smiles first
indulgently, then back at herself as child
beseechingly asking mom for her approval.

The woman she will be tells her that she's pretty
such a pretty girl, and the child she is
as the mother knows it too, she nods her head
and for that moment the three of them agree.

For the Executive Director of the Fallen

The little boy crying out
Weenie Weenie
in self-panicking delight,
waving his little cock
under the banner

of the sun, seemed pure Blake,
all anarchy and energy,
an innocence unfrightened
of itself that shook the lake's
waters and unsettled

the strained composures
and appointed certainties
of whatever Absolute Speaker
had been ranting in my brain:
Peace Through Strength

Justice Must Be Ours—
so many demon faces
in the glass city.
Each pubic triangle
seemed, under the bathing suits,

to grow electrical and crackle
with a sexual shock
that made me turn my face away:
and who should be there
but you, my dear Lord of Misrule,

blowing smoke in all our faces,
the clean bullet-hole in your forehead
above your self-ironic smile:
Don't let the monkeys
stop typing—

and after I swam
and I was sitting on the bank,
after the boy and his parents
had packed up and gone home,
I played the Noh play over for you

in the tape loop of the void
where your voice and laughter
so casually reside:
how the mother
gone searching for her

missing son finds him dancing
by the lake, and as she tries
to hold him he slips through
her arms just as she slips
through his arms—

and as she cries out
in perfect pitch in perfect time
to the shrieking bamboo flute
that her boy has drowned
she understands that she too

has drowned, that she too
is a ghost returning
to dance as they
dance together in a tighter
and tighter round.

Revenant

1

I light one cigarette off the butt of another
in the deep quiet of the study that magnifies
the moment when two lovers come together
just after the bomb hits and their bodies

in the cellar, in God knows what excesses of emotion,
turn sculptural, frozen in their last position.
To think like this used to make me queasy—
but then the thoughts become your body,

your face half-lit by whiskey
cutting through my shtick of mourning,
your laugh implying I'm an idiot for pretending
you're alive . . . and then you let my lips brush yours,

you almost meet my stare, face blushing
to the tips of your pale sensitive ears.

2

What really happened in the cellar?
You can hear the aftershock still echoing
in sun slanting through scorched mortar
piled higher than my head. I keep straying

into forbidden zones, body on top of body
hurled about in a mock orgy. Something like that—
it's stupid, in bad taste, narcissistically
transparent, but I can't not see you separate

from how we did what we did: you were always the one
for the big gesture, your politics and erotics
shouting back at you from scraped bare stone
at the swimming club you took me to, the Pigeon Rocks

foaming over as we balanced above the water
in the uneasy off-balance of the other.

3

You hold the too ripe orange up to the light
and smell the flesh, then peel it
in five pieces, juice stinking on your fingers,
sticky and sickly sweet, the rind's acid vapors

like your voice sweetly hectoring, whispering
what a fool I am, still living the life I'm shown,
not seeing, not understanding, not undertaking
to change what makes me so touchingly American,

my skeptical embrace of all viewpoints at once
when really, you can only thoroughly fuck
one lover, one cause, one enemy at a time. The trick's
to do it all sincerely, to make your allegiances

a form of love . . . Juice dribbles down your chin,
your mouth full of orange peel, fire, and sun.

4

The official report said it was a massacre.
The bomb exploded at approximately 2:45 a.m.
and was followed ten minutes later by another.
You were there, taking on the soul of a cat, and came

slinking by my elbow, butting and rubbing
your head against my skin, your paws
kneading and nicking me with just a show of claws,
your six toes the agreed on sign that this was you coming

back to me, your tail twitching with that sexy,
oh-so-impatient, let's-get-down-to-it come-on.
And then you lay down on my chest, your throaty,
deep purr rumbling so loud the explosion

faded out and all I could smell and all I could breathe
was your hot, damp breath breathing into my mouth.

Pig from Ohio

If you're a pig from Ohio,
all muscle and gristle,
not knowing they're planning
to rend you into bacon,

what better place
to find a wallow
than this blue-black mud
where you can keep yourself cool

as you wait for David
from Williamsfield, Ohio,
Sergeant in the Army's
4th Infantry—

two thousand-
six-hundred-fifty-seventh
casualty whose shadow
gets swallowed

in the 16 acre, 70 foot
hole that floats
on the Late Edition's
verso: the pig squeals

from the front page
smearing on fingers
of subway riders
who hear the echoes

through earth-movers
roaring all day
all night to fill the hole.
David, last name

Gordon, killed
in combat
by an IED
blasting through the armor

of his smoked Humvee,
David, take these slops
and shove them
in the pink face

and lashless eyes,
the slung belly's
sensual repose—
the good-natured maw

spreads wide as the air
as it squeals and drums
delicate trotters
in the swine fandango

a pig from Ohio
dances in time
to its appetite
that knows no better

than to bite
and bite
through wire,
cans, bones.

A Wedding at Cana, Lebanon, 2007

He said, "It is terrible what happens."
      And "So, Mr. Tom,
do not forget me"—an old-fashioned ring, pop tunes,
salsa! salsa! the techno-version of Beethoven's
Fifth, Fairouz singing how love has arrived,
that's what he heard after they dropped the bombs,
his ambulance crawling through smoke while cellphones
going off here here here kept ringing—
how the rubble-buried bodies' still living
relatives kept calling to see who survived.

And when he dug through concrete scree scorched black
      still smoking
from the explosion, squadrons of jets droning overhead,
houses blown to rebar, he saw cellphones'
display lights flashing from incoming calls
and when he flipped the covers, saw phone camera pics,
pics of kids, wives, dads, single, grouped, some wearing
silly party hats, scenes of hilarity
compacted on the screen: it was "not good"
he said, to have to take the phone out of the body

part pocket: *Hello—no, no, he's here,*
      right here, but not—
and then he'd have to explain . . . and so he stopped
answering. A soft-spoken young man
studying engineering, only moonlighting
as an ambulance driver, he stood at
the crossroads where Jesus turned water
into wine and where, rising out of rubble, floating down
the cratered street, bride and bridegroom came walking
in the heat and as they came the wedding guests held up

cell cameras clicking when the couple climbed, waving,
        into TRUST TAXI
blazoned on the car's rear windscreen. The muezzin's
nasal wail began to blare all over town, and the pair
drove off to ululating shouts and cries, firecrackers
kicking up dust in the square. The show over, we
got back into our car, our tires crunching
over rubble. As I sat there rubbernecking
at a burned-out tank, he shrugged: "All this—how embarrassing."
And "I hope this is the story you are after."

Reporter

Please, don't let me die this way: up all night
to file a story, drinking too much
so I fall asleep at lunch, dreaming
how my life runs backward
back to the mountain's shadow I grew up in,
my bike racing downhill while the maniac Hitler
sits watching pornography down in his bunker,
doing something halfway normal at least.

How I wanted to live life in the newsreels,
how I've loved and kept on loving the adrenaline high . . .

You feel part of history, history opens in the night to you,
history takes you in like no lover ever can.

How sick I've been, the infection of hearing voices always
at war . . . soldiers talking the way they do
in sports metaphors, while I shrink myself
to nothing just to feel history and my nothing
come together in the most beautiful fucking
you can't quite feel—
                              it's like a blue movie
where no one ever comes and if you get tired
all you have to do is run
the movie backward and shadows racing up
to kill each other rewind like lovers
walking backward out the bedroom door.

My darling bending over me
hates to see me like this—fallen asleep again
from too much wine. I'm useless, helpless,
my eyeglasses shining in the sea light in the open air restaurant.
She wants to make me understand that she gave her youth to me
just as I gave my youth to her:
but what does that giving mean
if she's eternally young, even if she misses me—her drunk old man.

"This Thing of Darkness"

On YouTube, you can watch a cell phone video of Saddam Hussein's execution. The sound quality and the resolution are poor: the voices in the room reverberate like pieces of metal clanging together, Saddam's footsteps, as he climbs what look like steel stairs to the scaffold, echo too loudly, the execution chamber, if that is what it is, distorts every noise in babbling over-and-undertones that resonate like the acoustics of an indoor swimming pool.

Whoever is holding the cell phone—and it is my hunch that it is Shakespeare, since who else could write such a scene in which Saddam's lavish rhetoric and defiant presence could exact from its audience this precise mixture of horror, sadness, joyous vindication, and disgust—seems under constraint to keep the phone hidden from the authorities in the room; and so making a virtue out of his necessities, Shakespeare succeeds in building the scene's tension by showing it from the perspective of someone whose moral sensibilities are revolted by the spectacle but who can't tear his eyes away. The room jiggles in the lens, ceiling and floor buck and roll, everything feels murkily contingent, the graininess of the footage both brutal and cliched.

Now Saddam has mounted the steps, and stands with his arms bound behind him on the trap door beneath his feet, his black coat making the salt and pepper in his beard more evident. Now Shakespeare keeps the lens steadily focussed on Saddam's upper body, as if the guards, in their fascination with the coming execution, have relaxed their vigilance: Saddam's broad shoulders, the shovel-blade beard, the broad forehead and intense, sunken eyes make him seem larger than life . . . but also paltry, foolish, cruelly paternal—and also a little stagy, as if he were hamming it up for the camera. As he denounces his enemies, the steadiness of Shakespeare's focus brings the soundtrack into focus: Saddam's voice is clear, forceful, though the acoustics exaggerate it so much that it's difficult to separate his voice from the distortions boomeranging off the room's concrete ceiling and walls.

But the picture itself is suddenly steady and clear: the symmetrical, snugged up knots of the hangman's noose, eight loops in all, the sense of the rope as having recently been bought by an experienced hand, well acquainted with the requirements of nooses, their tensile strength and resistance to a body that weighs between 180 and 185 pounds and that will fall through a drop of 15 feet in order to snap the neck with instantaneous force, these are the focus in everyone's eyes, guards, executioner, reporters, visiting officials, post-factum experts and jabberers.

And, of course, in Shakespeare's eyes—Shakespeare, who must find all this horribly familiar, but promising material. One can already sense him spinning out lines of dialogue, not the official statements, but what the distracted guards are thinking: one who is still secretly loyal to Saddam sees him as a stalwart, unrepentant, defiant martyr in his last moments, a Coriolanus denouncing the mob that will murder him; and others, whose families have been tortured and murdered, can be heard crying out: "Tear him to pieces, do it presently:—he killed my son;—my daughter;—he killed my cousin Marcus;—he killed my father—."

And now Richard III steps up beside Saddam, and then Titus and Macbeth and Lear also step forward to take their places around the doomed man, even as the guards offer Saddam a hood that he refuses. They edge in closer together, shoulder to shoulder, and stand there draping their arms around Saddam and one another: and as the photo op begins its Ariel-like, digital girdling of the globe, they grow into their full stature as villians, tyrants, homicides, noble, rhetorical, thinkingly or unthinkingly cruel, all imagining themselves more sinned against than sinning. . . . They gesture to Shakespeare to step up onto the stage of the scaffold and take a bow, but Shakespeare refuses, he stays down in the pit among the groundlings, filming up from below at Saddam either cursing his captors or joining in with what sounds like a prayer just before the executioner springs the trap door: and in that moment you can hear History or Revenge or Judgment saying:

Set him breast deep in earth, and famish him;
There let him stand, and rave, and cry for food;
If any one relieves or pities him,
For the offence he dies. This is our doom:
Some stay to see him fasten'd in the earth.

And in response:

O, why should wrath be mute and fury dumb?
I am no baby, I, that with base prayers
I should repent the evils I have done:
Ten thousand worse than ever yet I did
Would I perform, if I might have my will . . .

And then the trap door is sprung, and there is a dark smudgy blur that is
Saddam falling, and a kind of howling and clanking and tangling of voices
murmuring, shouting, crying out, an idiot hubbub reverberating against me-
tallic shudderings and bangings that go on and on—and then all drowned in
blackness, blackness, blackness: Shakespeare up to his old tricks, even with
a shitty cell phone video? Was the darkness so great under the scaffold that
the lens couldn't pick out Saddam, neck snapped, body dangling, limp? Well,
Shakespeare knows how to make a moment dramatic—more and more fran-
tically, the viewer keeps peering into the blackness, trying to make sense of
what has happened: did they finish the job? Is Saddam dead? Is all that blither
and babble assaulting one's ears like the noise of the storm gathering in Lear's
mind: "Blow, winds, and crack your cheeks!" Or is it simply the stampede of
officialdom beginning to vacate the chamber while the doctor certifies that
yes, the pulse is stopped, subject died at such and such a time, disposition and
disposal of corpse to take place according to plan . . .

Later, after viewing the video back in his room, Shakespeare concludes that the overall effect is crude, but the scene builds well, the rhetoric carries the day, and that the blackout is an excellent device—more effective, in the end, than the actual showing of the body. After all, everybody has seen hundreds upon hundreds of corpses, if not in real life, then on TV, at the movies, in books, in plays. No, a corpse doesn't have nearly the dramatic force that it used to have . . . and he remembers back to when he was a boy working as a butcher, exercising his father's trade, that when he killed a calf he would do it in high style, and make a speech. And everyone would laugh, the calf would be skinned out, the meat salted—and then the next one would stumble up, be tied down, and made ready for the knife.

But still, there was something about the speech itself, separate from the calf, and even one's own voice, that made it seem like a gesture of respect toward the poor, helpless creature about to be killed. It was worth a few words, after all. Even this bootleg version of Saddam's death—titillating, almost cheaply pornographic in its forbidden, smuggled out quality—can't help but remind Shakespeare of the cardinal rule of his profession: don't bore the audience, even if you have to throw in some mindless violence or gratuitous sex. This is something an old pro understands: it's not enough to use the imagination as a form of insider privilege to give you access to the scene of an historic execution. Take it from Will Shakespeare, former butcher's boy and glover, you've got to skin and tan it with your own mind before you can relish it, deplore it.

A Promise

"An Italian citizen of Jewish race"
Has written, "The need for *lavoro ben fatto*—
Work done well—is so deep as to induce
People to perform even slave labor properly." And so

A promise is kept, a pen meets paper,
And the laws of perspective that hide
The lesser pain behind the greater
Begin to order the words that confide

To the screen *Babelturm, Bobelturm*—
Our own latter day Tower of Babel rising
From the Lager's mud in a soft spring storm,
Pipes, rails, boilers dripping, scaffolding gleaming

Round the carbide tower of the rubber factory,
Not transcendent or divine, but inherent,
Historical, built of *brick, briques, Ziegel, cegli* . . .
And so the tower follows the blueprint

Of the skilled hands that draw each line and angle—
And for those who think it up, the tower rules the air
While out in the freezing three-dimensional
The one whose trowel dresses each brick with mortar

Places it, by hand, in sturdily laid rounds: "So he
Who loathed Germans, their language, their war,
Built their walls straight and solid, because to be
Their slave made him love his work even more."

Hunter Gatherer

after Ellen Driscoll's art installation "Hunter Gatherer"

1

Snow falling on the roof falls like it used to do
when freeze and thaw hardened to a satin-sheen
and nothing moved in the offing but the lighthouse beam.

And so this morning is the morning of the heart
in which the vodka, talking shit all night,
dissolves into pure sunlight, purer thought,

and I'm not a whore and I'm not a bastard
and I wake clear-headed and see
above the clouds like a swept bare prison yard

each cool hard instant of nothing but blank sky.
No sound of the All Clear, no need for intensity
or all the fake drama of some TV war. Just the eye

of the ocean staring through a neighbor's window
with a sense of absolution no one younger can ever know.

2

Your snipers crouch on rooftops, your oil derricks
and McMansions gleam . . . you made it all from plastic,
scrounging water bottles at dawn with the other derelicts

and then cutting and gluing in the studio
your own slum of alabaster, your shining city
on the hill. Remember when I told you

in my aspiring bad boy way, how I found
in a footnote to *Plymouth Plantation*
the dissenter put to death with the cow he sodomized?

As if I'd made a dare, your eyes met mine,
then you went back to your drawing, your concentration,
now made perfect, cutting me down to size.

And the brown and blue ink flowing from your hand
mingled into lines only the ink could intend.

3

I want to see you put on those boots again,
those ones we bought from the Farmer's Co-op
to tramp around mud-spattered fields.

I want to see you bend down and shove your toe
and thick sock into that green rubber sleeve
sheathing your foot and calf up to the knee

while you lean against me to steady your balance,
the two of us braced against each other
in sway and countersway, trust moving against chance

but nothing more at stake than what was always
at stake, life making its extensions,
then pulling back away—there we go across the water meadows

in slip and slop, hand in hand to see the manor house
the lord and lady pulled the roof off against the taxes.

4

Light plashes down on your white plastic plain—
and no one knows the end, or how this war comes out,
or who's a casualty and who's not:

Your snipers take aim. Rifles gleam in the spotlights.
Your shanty towns transfigure into lustrous flows
of shadow that make the enemy hard to spot:

everything is camouflaged in light,
in hard-to-see-through veils of glare and dazzle.
And then the first shot's fired and in the split-second lull

before light explodes itself against light
and every light goes out, I see your careful silhouette,
head cocked to the side measuring the effect

of just how far is too far, how close too close
before such warring luminosities turn friend into foe.

After a Rembrandt Motif

Nightmare dog, little mutt, little stray, doing something

you shouldn't, you hunker down in someone's foreground
shitting while the hours while away in the whoever whatever

wherever of nails and cross, vinegar sponge, the hours spent

up there looking down on you, doing what you
do, digging for something, bones, food?

A demon of unknowing unknown to you looks out through

your eyes at the hanging three, begging for a handout, tail wagging
impervious to their agony that isn't anyway anything to do with

food or being scratched where that bastard flea, right

there, behind the ear, keeps you itching itching.
Hand on the leash chokeholding you yanks you back from vomit,

feces, lusciously stinking corpses. What is that thing

you're holding in your black-gummed smile?
And why are all the dogs all over town digging in that mound?

Come here, fetch, roll over, sit up, shake, stay, play dead.

And while the anointed one tells an astonished crowd
the meaning of a dream that will save the nation,

you put your head between your legs and lick.

The Games

1/ Morning News

Mist drifting above wheel ruts and matted salt hay
blinks back the first mild delusion of the day:
your voices locked in friendly combat out in the arena
of mud and marshgrass where a hermit crab, one huge claw

held high, plays the gladiator with a dying gull,
scuttling with its kind in the stink of engine oil.
Both of you connived at the martyr's role,
your dueling letters to the editor

a life and death struggle though nobody
now knows what thumbs up or down means.
So in these lines let me try to keep you near

while clarities of air rise up against the stones
of our crumbling colliseums when the IED
blows the bus fifty feet into the air.

2/ At the Party

You were throwing a party when the phone
rang to say he'd been shot at point-blank range,
but all through the evening you didn't let on,
just kept smiling . . . his photo on your desk trained

its gaze on us who as yet knew nothing,
though we knew you, our host, was dying—you, veiled
in your hundred courtesies, a different one
for each of us, the seasoned diplomat juggling

our need for you to be now vulnerable,
now brave, now hopeful, now resigned . . . or smiling
and nodding among servants, retainers, whores,

the Etruscan master in his painted tomb
gesturing for more wine, unshaken by the bombs,
while the *hors d'oeuvres* keep coming round forever.

3/ The Sack

The lord of the dead rests one hand on your shoulder
and his other holds his hammer, guarding the door
to the other world from which a breeze blows
though it's only salt air through beach house windows

as you keep plunging into the waters of your own party
and come out soaked in our pregnant glances,
part concern, part voyeurism (Look, he's dying!),
part fearful satisfaction that your cancer isn't ours.

And now, long after the party when I think of how
they forced him to crawl into a sack just before they
shot him so he'd be easier to dump into the sea

here he comes barging in on your elegy, Rabelaisian
and sweaty, rodomontading about how he detests politics
and anyone who'd die for something dumb as an idea.

4/ A Citizen of the Empire

300 dead bears and 300 dead lions,
not bad for one morning, though we're hoarse
from shouting and hungry for lunch during the noon
executions, the higher class criminals

crucified, the slaves and Christians being mauled
by leopards, though what we're really waiting for
are the gladiator fights in the afternoon.
And once the sand is bloody and the corpses

hauled away, we'll bow to the gods and rise
to go home—but not before we pile in carts
some of the lion and bear steaks that the Emperor

has decreed the imperial butchers
carve for us: roast bear is my favorite,
but roast lion, especially the flanks, can be delicious.

5/ Portents

But once the games die out and before the next ones start,
when it comes time to sober up, who will take notice
of dire portents, what the auguries predict?
Chasms spitting fire. Rain showering blood. Mice

eating gold. Meanwhile, the clear light
keeps falling on Constantine's marble foot,
bigger than a tank, that keeps on treading down
us Gauls, Germans, Volscians, who pray to Christ and Woden

and look both ways when Caesar makes us citizens.
Then the games become our games, our enemies
the same as the centurions burning out our former brothers

far away on the frontiers where trees
still bleed, bird-men rustle feathers, and one-eyed Arimaspians
fight the griffins for their treasure.

6/ Marsh at Low Tide: After Signorelli's *Last Judgment*

If, as he painted it, eyes stare up out of the underlife
and ghostly forms shed floods of emptiness
until as flesh emergent they push themselves
head first through the earth of their own graves,

springing out skin and bone to walk on heaven's soil,
then what could I say to make these cattails
and marshgrass blowing all one way
fecund as the shiftings in this generating clay

so you too could lift yourselves up out of mud,
muscular torsos and clear eyes going lighter at the sight
of your own naked sexes flushed with blood.

Powder burns and wounds and scars all healed, you'd levitate
above the demons whose asses, shoved in our faces,
burn the flame-green of the bending reeds.

Spell

from the Greek Magical Papyri

The spell was the spell of words half-heard,
syllables jumbled in a language that was
animal and sexual, moans overheard,
creaks and groans turning to gunshots
and back again, the window's blankness offering
no resting place, nothing to link with:
I wasn't his wife, lover, daughter repeating
the spell that would keep the spell from having
to be repeated, as if the words were a tongue
speaking beyond anybody's will to stop
what it was saying:
                    If I'd seen him stretched
out in a hotel bed, beard soft and tangled,
wrists knobby as a teenage girl's, mouth
soft, straight out of Cavafy, I'd have
said he floated in post-coital sleep . . .
but his breath when they yanked off his hood
had stopped and what his hand gripped
wasn't his lover's shoulder but a machine pistol:
*Don't look beneath the waist: that's where
the bomb made a martyr of him . . .*
Where I walked on the sea front two days ago,
a car bomb blackened the swimming club
and killed a Beirut politician and his brother.
I felt myself at the edge of the big story:
there was something so soft about his body
as he lay there, open to all comers,
stalled forever in the climax of his pleasure.
I had no rights in him at all, and yet there I was

in my words' oily sheen, ready to cover
him over, lave him . . .

                  Now, a big wind
blows the door wide open and light
streams in as church bells bong
to a voice in the bedrock deep
under the pulpit:

              Barking dog, by those who hung
themselves, by all those stabbed, shot, blown up,
by all the bruised and bloodied dead and by
the holy head of the infernal god,
bring my love to me, bring him
back to me before this dog stops barking.

Yellow caution tape declaiming in Arabic
and English
          STAY BACK

TWO

To Death

You won't wipe away my joy

in my seaweed skin, my hunched neck,
my folds and creases you hide in
even as I throw my arm around you and lie

my leg sweaty and cooling next to yours.
I know you make my face more
interesting to me on this beautifully

lit stage made to look like an open
field where I wander in your theater
of fantasies touching God knows what

in this delirium of bodies
in this noisy club where everybody's
drinking and that's you leaning over

secretly spitting in everybody's drink.

The Chosen One

The embarrassment of wanting to pray to God,
the demand that God give a good Goddamn

had made him pretty nutty by the end; a lifelong Marxist,
he took up with Ouspensky, then spent all his money

(and he had tons, all those years in the bank
when *Das Kapital* and the *Wall Street Journal*

vied for subway reading time) on learning Gurdjieff
Sufi dances, spinning round and round in an ecstasy

of sweating, chanting, his happiness making him
call you on the phone to tell you in a way that made you

wince that he loved you for your holiness, regardless
of your failings that he would then go on to list

in rigorous, half humorous detail. But now, he was dying,
and dying fast, and he was pissed; pissed at life, more pissed

at death, most pissed at us, his useless fucking friends,
hangdog, silent under his scorn, withstanding his tongue-lashings,

then withdrawing to email, messages left on his machine.
And through it all, only his little dog, a white terrier

named Constanza, escaped his vitriol, his mortified, lacerating,
self-annihilating rages set off, so he said, by God's hatred,

God's malice, God's need to get his hooks in you
and twist you and turn you until His bullying was satisfied.

And while he was saying this, his hand would drift down
past the bedrails and immediately she was there,

licking his fingers, looking up with complete canine
accomodation, the reassuring tail wagging undismayed

by the smell beginning to come off him. It was as if God
put the dog in the room to uncover his friends as paltry

Job's comforters, in an accursed experiment to show
how isolated death can make a man, so that only

a dumb creature could be avid in its love, rising up
as we fell down in the scale of his affections;

and how he gave himself to that tongue, its absorbed,
infantile bliss, the dog up on her hind legs

coming out of her dogginess to meet him coming out
of his God cursed pain: her tongue slathered

and slurped his pungently acrid,
irresistible salts, the soon to be carrion salts

that gave to him such flavor—he, her chosen one,
his skin and smell enveloping her in lusciously novel

stinks and savors, as if only now was he the chrism, the oil
her dog-hearted devotions had so long thirsted for.

For a Spacesuit Set Adrift

> *NASA had reported that the "SuitSat" device [a Russian spacesuit equipped with a radio transmitter and stuffed with old clothes that was set adrift from the International Space Station] had ceased working within hours of its release on Friday. But a US amateur radio spokesman said weak signals had been picked up. "Death reports were premature," he said.*
>
> —*BBC*

1

Under the starflood
where the flood of earth confronts her,
tiny, unmoored, drifting upside down,
the ocean's pupil peers into her helmet's faceplate:

voices hiss and crackle . . . *too late . . . your fault . . .*
It's not what she did but what she did
not do that haunts her.

Ears ache with intonations calling
from dimensions beyond the three she knows
where the dead come and go,
where absurd consolations talk inside her helmet.

Who gave the order that made her take this walk
past the corner comet, the next door asteroid?
Why, why was she shoved out into this void?

2

Think of mayhem out in space, matter-hungry black holes
that flay their stellar neighbors, fields of gravitation
that crush matter to nearly nothing, galaxies
colliding and eating one another—

all of it going on in invisible bands of the spectrum
nobody at a funeral is aware of in the music,
in the way the mourner leans over the coffin and strokes the wood.

Marooned where nobody can reach her,
her abandonment expanding like the decimals of pi,
she senses the dead approaching, here, here—
the dead that the ones down there

glued to their antennae so desire and fear.
They shove her out the airlock, they shove her out again,
again the void fills her suit the way it fills the dark she floats in.

3

No way through, no way out but this:
or so say the ones that track her
while earth crackles with a plea
please please don't ever leave me

But voices of the dead decay
into babble of the radio bubble
spreading ever wider and deeper into space.

The split second delay between when their mouths open
and the sound reaches her ear
takes the measure of her already changed position
as if all she needs to do is step out into the tenth dimension

where her old dresses and blouses come to life once more—
but space curls and curves away . . .
How she loathes infinity. She moves where the void moves her.

4

She dreams of the mothership.
She dreams of gravity.
She dreams space as her unbrokenness,
her body touching everywhere.

She's back before the big bang,
before anyone can laugh at her,
before her body can abandon her

and love drifts away.
She forgets past and future,
she doesn't grow older or younger,
no tears distort her eyes.

Her ears are closed to everything.
Every signal is decayed.
All space compresses into her smile.

O. D.

I was surprised to find them
parading their deaths in front of me,
teenage Banquos grinning, insinuating,
snapping their fingers
in a cliché of cool,
dancing, sly, refusing to lie
down and be buried
under pity,
           high-school kids racing
to the edge not knowing
every step
sheers away
into a precipice—
           but they mocked
my solemnity, shoved off my pity,
my anger and sadness
annoyed them, they were tougher
than I'd imagined—
           Danny,
playing his saxophone, improvised
around the circle of fifths,
his tall, slender body
standing square-shouldered
as he blew and blew;
and the other boy, Peter,
he holds his guitar
defensively in front of him,
he wards off all comers,
he wraps around
himself a wall of electric *wha-wha*—.

Not quite boys, not quite men
doing to themselves
what death does to you—courting
some out of bounds sensation
pushing back into the vein
up the arm to the heart
rushing to the brain:
one was found by his mother
slumped in the bathtub's
cooling water, the other
lying curled on himself
like a wild creature, foetally
drawn up, shoes off,
shoe lace tied around his bicep.

Long hair bouncing
on their shoulders, dancing,
dancing, their bodies
not quite grown into,
they project attitude
that charms and
cuts all ways—
they seem unaware
of pain, their concerns
aren't long term,
they look sexually turned on
and rigorously absorbed
the way a mother
with her newborn looks, feeding,
feeding, their faces shine,
their eyes say OK OK OK
they are doing for themselves

what we do
for ourselves, lively hunters
and gatherers risking
what they are, they walk out
of themselves into the lives
they now live by not living.

Money

Two drinks down, and there's money
begging to be fucked by me, to fuck me silly,
money's hand clutching at my sleeve—
foolishly aware of how money must rave

all over the city, demanding, begging,
telling lies I need to hear and money
needs to tell. It's ridiculous and sad,
this wanting sharpening money's naked need

as if money were a cock, a cunt that can't stop
coming, and the more it comes the more
it has to come, money money money
making me feel what I can't shut down enough

not to feel in this wanting of not
having I have to have even as I have it.

Fenix

1

Face cross-hatched by violet shadows that fall round her like a net,
she struggles through steel walls to squeeze back
onto the street just before I wake, as if an unknown planet,

cross-currenting earth's gravity, tugged her harder, harder:
Planet Pizza Crust, Planet Souvlaki Scrap,
Planet of Her Little House of Cardboard on the Corner,

Planet of Her Little House of Rain When It Rains.
She seems almost to swim, her legs on one side of the detention
center's walls, her head and shoulders bursting

through the other: tagged in white paint on the steel doors:
Dios es amor: and then she slides
on through, exhaust fumes shawling round her shoulders.

2

I'd wake, she'd fade: and all through my walk to work, threading
hi-rise grids of Cor-Ten steel, I'd feel my grip, in that planet's
influence, slipping off my lower rung; or like swaying on an I-beam

80 stories high, could I freefall as far as her?
—Face shoving through the dream, bundled in holey sweaters
and men's sweatpants bulging with newspaper

to keep warm, she'd stare right through the lady cops
threatening to shoo her off—but just as often turning a blind eye
while she sat selling crayons loose from the box,

scratched bottles of nail polish, tattered books and magazines,
even a beret. Once, a draggled kitten
peeked its head out from her coat. Once I saw a man trying

to hit her, her screaming back, *Get your pinche shit*
away from me, pinche culero—everyone looking
away until the beat cops happened by and broke it up.

And once I saw her coming out of the detention center's
cable-gridded doors: escorted by a guard,
she shrugged eyebrows in greeting; I smelled her odor,

laminar as wet spring dirt giving off leaf-rot,
urine tang, sweetish, acrid mellowing of dried feces:
there was something stolid, pugnacious even in her jaw's jut

that shoved past barriers; yet she held aloof, caught
behind her own fragile walls, eyes signalling *Posted No Trespassing*
to mine. And behind that depth of silence, what?

3

"Underclass" "street people" "homeless" "the poor"—
as if such terms didn't dull the gleam, amidst cratered concrete,
of the mother-of-pearl butterfly comb holding back her hair,

her own sense of her inside different than the eyes that looked at her,
no matter the seamed lines raying her mouth and eyes,
mascara smudged; as if the city's lights could afford her nothing more

than her little busted lawnchair tethered to a single square of ungiving
sidewalk . . . but of course I knew, my dream made sure
I knew, the real nature of that illumination: her face keeps dissolving

into the detention center's floodlights sanding smooth her features
even as she tries to hoard what she can against that glare: and as I give
her a quarter, the dream envelops me, she bends down to where

I huddle in a ratty sleeping bag, walkie-talkie voices crackling in my ear
Move Move as I lie there, unable to flinch a muscle.
And now she's saying, what, she wants a dollar?

And the dream fading out, I'm shaking my head "no" with that little
annoyed shake that says, "who are you to me"
as our eyes swim away even as we exchange strained smiles . . .

4

Soon after that, I saw her counting spare change into
her drink holder, her face shining an angry orange:
jaundice, I remember thinking, she's for it now:

and two weeks later, she was gone: maybe she moved to another part
of the city, but I'd seen that same orange
on a friend's face just days before he died . . . Weeks after that,

I couldn't walk by that spot without thinking how "Fenix"—
the name the dream called her, I never knew her real name—was still
there: so that when I neared the corner I couldn't help but tense

a block or so away and grip whatever spare change I had,
knowing it wasn't enough even as I tried not knowing, ready to trigger
loose my coins and nod, with feigned ease, to her nod . . .

And even now, in that tension that makes her absence
present, her atoms seem to leave a trace
some sixth sense in me feels the way planets

feel the gravitation of black holes:
I see her at the edge of all that energy being sucked
into anti-matter feet first because gravity pulls

slightly stronger on her toes. And without really thinking
any of it's there, I see the rickety, flashing wheels of her laundry cart.
I see her hand thrust out, face unreadable, gone wooden, gaze pointing

at my chest right at heart level. And most of all I see her sunglasses
that say in florid cursive on one tinted lens *Kiss*
and on the other lens *My Ass*.

Round

Somebody's alone in his head, somebody's a kid,
somebody's arm's getting twisted—a sandwich flies apart,

tomatoes torn, white bread flung, then smeared with shit
and handed back to eat—*I dog dare you, I double dog dare you* . . .

Somebody's watching little shit friends watch little shit him
climb to the crown of a broken-down cherry tree

and throw cherries at him: now somebody's pushing
somebody into a sprinkler, everyone's laughing, everyone's shouting

in that frenzy when a buddy's gonna get hurt,
gonna get mad, gonna swing and swing from the top of the sky—

somebody's falling through trees shedding leaves,
October light you can see through,

somebody can't read the menu, can't find his glasses,
can't remember most mornings his best friends' names—

somebody's racing just ahead of what it means to be "it,"
porch lights coming on, trees jumping out at him,

and that nameless smell, smell of the highschool lunchroom
mingled with formaldehyde when somebody does dissections,

frog legs strangely human under the fine-edged scalpel,
keeps making somebody waken, not certain anymore

of what window, which door, voices fading to a spectral
whine in somebody's ears, eyes calm, clear, the starpoint steeple

piercing somebody's brain moving alone through mist, darkness, rain,
somebody's eye's, somebody's mouth cooling, hardening to bronze.

Triumph

My mother, sure, everything I know
is from my mother. She told me stories about
being a schoolteacher in a one-room schoolhouse
in a prairie town so isolated her father and she drove
right through it and never noticed.
The loneliness, she said, of living in that town,
of boarding at the home of one of her students—
the loneliness was the kind where you keep
telling yourself, *This won't kill me*
and if it does, then I won't know it, I'll be dead.
That made it go away for a while,
though you can't ever forget it: it's the voice
under the voice of every casual word.
I can hear it now when she's reproachful on the phone—
she's in a Poe story, the walls are moving in,
and in the middle of the floor there's a pit, a drop
into darkness a thousand feet down.
—The old drama queen. But she's also got that mad nobility
in her voice that makes me imagine her
riding like a Roman General on her horse through
everything she's been through, my father's death,
her children's cutting silences, her hardscrabble childhood
on the farm when they lived on 50 cents a day
and once, when she dropped the money through the floorboards,
they had to pry them up so they wouldn't go hungry,
she's got her yo-yoing blood pressure, her adult onset diabetes,
the numbness in her feet, and fatigue that makes her feel
like she can't keep on but she does keep on,
she plays the piano, chords from her Fake Book
That Old Devil Moon, I've Got You Under My Skin
and then she reads, reads late into the night
and that's when, at the edges of her mind a voice
comes creeping, a voice, sure, she's heard it before,

it's the voice that echoes out of ruins piling up
one stone at a time, until the rubble piles up to your neck—
but none of them notice, not even the old drunk soldiers
clinging to their dignity through you as you ride by,
they can't bear to see the rubble, they just see the horse,
and you, you keep up the show, you don't, for their sakes,
disappoint—just who the hell thought life has any style at all?—
and all the while, down among the mob, your son
stares up at you riding despite your wounds, the mob
of Rome shouting and applauding you in your triumph—
and behind you there follows, in accordance with the ritual,
a slave crying out, *Remember, you're nothing but a mortal.*

THREE

Speech for a Fly

Sticky-footed love, that's me: what isn't love's food
when your element is excrement and rot?
I go berserk battering myself against brightness,
I drop to the sill and mourn my shriveled brothers,

then live out my moment swerving between flyswatters
and your hundred hands flailing in my many eyes,
hands so angry, eager to hurt, but baby,
this fly isn't gonna make it easy.

Watch out for me smashing through air
as I come at you like a mugger around the corner:
I can kill a pope, make an emperor die,
I'm the little spark of fire that burns whole towns,

consumes the world entire, I'm the base worm
that devours honor, parents, sister, brother,
and at the last you'll be mine too. So endure
my touch on your cheek and arm,

come closer to my soul before my whine
winds down and I lie listless
on the sill, toppled on my back or rolled
into the emptiness between transparency and pane.

homage to Patrick Carey

Through the Lens

1

Not my childhood, not anyone's anymore—
a kid hangs himself and you find him dangling there
and everybody whispers when a girl gets pregnant—
or somebody's baby dies and the parakeet

she watched from her crib dies too.
Or the girl in the orchard kicking off her shoes,
scuffed like yours, when she pins you
and rolls and you pin her and roll, half the weeds

in the orchard get flattened down that way.
Cloud shadows glide over the mountains' rockslides
while a magnifying glass fries a grasshopper

in a canning jar and dirt clods she throws
bust up between your shoulderblades
and you duck away and want nothing bigger than what's there.

2

Except for that parakeet, its little—feet? not
quite claws, the feel of them on your naked wrist
exciting, awful, scaly, like the baby
they made you hold—caught between

the bird's eye and the spaced out baby's:
it's almost funny the way the bird flies back
into your mind, baby and bird and girl confused,
baby in her crib, then her white satin coffin—

while the split, cracked lips of the girl brushes
against your ear and leaves a trickle of dried blood
next morning in the mirror to be picked at

like a scab over and over in a town, a street, a house
that in a hundred years will or won't be there,
though touched by its own kind of shut-mouthed despair.

3

Wherever I grew up, it doesn't exist,
it never existed, it was a fake, a movie set,
a place to be torn down once
the cameras stopped filming. And it's not

because you can't find it on a map. It's still there, off 80,
between a mountain range and valley
where that girl's vaccination mark flashes like silt
that flows through the irrigation ditches' sluice boards.

And whatever still holds its own against flirt
and heart-flicker, pure transience and fear, inscribes
itself in cloud shapes on walls of falling stone

that yell back to the schoolyard
and the blackened cage of the incinerator burning
fuckfuckfuck to snowed-in mountains.

4

It's all the ball the ball the ball
in impossible cut-backs and fakes
that make it keep going on after recess bell
and plus and minus and radical

dash across the blackboard while the square root
of pi's impossible disdain
neither notes your dirty shoes and grass-stained jeans
or wastes decimal dignity giving you

the time of day. But still you're in the flow,
gaining on infinity, still taking it
at face value while the classroom mumbles

with dust-ups and rebellions and pencils
scritching out answers whose wrongness proves
nothing the theorem didn't already know.

5

And while you bend to your work, your eraser
rubbing hard, all at once the paper
rips—and before you isn't a veil of the usual
torn open but a void through which you pass

like sunrays streaming through a magnifying glass
so that the paper burning a hole into itself
spasms up at its own center that ripples
outward and leaves nothing unchanged . . . except

in how your eyes dodge out to the never-end of numbers
where a voice whispers precepts
you can't quite hear—like that girl

whispering above you playing secrets
playing house *shh shh,* her bloody lip
against your ear rubbed rough as the paper's nap.

A Woman at a Table

1

For him, she can't not be her,
        not adept at being
                what the slight breeze
flowing between them
        wants to be: fluidly
shifting, refreshed
        until it dies away.
                        Dies away into
hands and gestures
and smiling grimaces,
              his breathing entering
her moaning—
        but now the breeze
turning to sweat
        sliding makes the woman
she is when bodies aren't
        intertwining keep on
sitting at a table,
        luxuriating in the moaning
while she's free
                to keep still
by the window and feel
the breeze cool between
        her fingers, strong,
                   always young, though not
like a young woman's hands, no.

2

Light sliding down
        table legs pools around
                the bodies moving

together but she's
        lifted far above them,
high on her own
        deception as if "no"
didn't exist
                for him while for her
"no" was what
allowed her
                to flow into
his shadow
        so that never
would her release
                from him
be known—her arms
                pulling him closer
as she drifts out from
        under him, leaving
him down there—
        as if she herself
were some other
woman come
        to take her
place in light and breeze
and shadow
                in the window . . .
and feeling light
        touch that face
approaching, she
                rises, she goes.

3

To a place where
        no one has ever
                come to find her.
Where instincts are
        like junkyard dogs
who bark and bark,
        and so she pats
each head until
                each lies down, rolls
over, and plays
                    dead.
It's like she
        wanted to make sex
something other
        than grunts
and sentiment.
        To make it
stand for itself without
                pandering to the heart.
To dress her lust
        in something sheer
enough that she
        can see right
through it to the way
        he makes her feel
so wayward
        in her nakedness,
so out there beyond
                his smile

that what she
                needs isn't him
or her or whatever
        words they're
calling out but
        the flicker
back and forth of
        being hers and
his and hers.

On First Avenue and Sixth Street

There are days the whole world gets down on all fours;
if you're twenty or sixty, you'd do it in an alley,
                bodies thrown together—
and when it's over, one or both of you stumbling
                out into afternoon, ghosting
                        through air it goes
                                on and on . . .
The absence that starts to shine on Atlantic Avenue,
                        the crazy drive-by
            joy that turns the speakers so loud the car
                vibrates now becomes years later
a story you tell your child who grows up to be a Veejay
                in a dance club
                over in Williamsburg.
The East River where you used to walk in Carl Schurz Park
                        looks like it drags
into the current's weave the Domino Sugar Factory,
silo architecture on fire in the oily spangle
that joins the Hudson upstream at Spuyten Duyvil.

                The world gets down on all fours
                        and that's you
yelling your head off as a boy, pounding your mitt,
            the grass not quite grown in because its April
and the odors wafting up are dogshit and leafrot,
                        spunk buried in winter muck
                        releasing head clearing
effluvium, sky overarcing the batting cage
            and chainlink backstop, home plate's white diamond
making a satisfying thump womp when you pound
            your bat three times as you step up to the plate:
                        out there in the river
            a pirate was flung from the yardarm,

and that's where the giant ape
clung, beating his chest bloodied by machine guns
of the gnat-sized Curtiss Helldivers
his giant, seamed hand
bats from the sky.
Or the mushroom blast looms up in the boxed-in screen
and radiation transmogrifies
crabs become the size
of boxcars that charge you from their cave
where they discuss your fate
in the voices of mad scientists
they've just eaten.

This is the day when the world
gets down on all fours, and you and she lie out on the city beach,
sun dazzle in the shallows, tinflash on the far swell
as the thieving Parking Meter Czar
slashes his wrists
upstairs while talking to his shrink,
his wife listening in
too late on the extension downstairs . . . for the wife
a tragedy,
but for the two of you chuckling
at the headline,
Corrupt Meter Man Expires,
weren't you happier
back then, tuned in to radio waves beamed out across the universe,
the song's last word reversed
the first word alien ears would hear, *whole lotta love*
evol attol elohw
the radio bubble widening 100 light years through space
broadcasting Led Zeppelin, Cream, Zappa's
"Weasels Ripped My Flesh"

inspiring your own vodka-fueled arias
                never heard in the high clamshell hall
                listening to the woman without
                        a shadow
        sing to the unborn children singing
in the frying pan their lovely sorrow at not being born:
                don't let yourself be turned
                        to stone
        like the Emperor who can only be saved
                if his wife, Empress of the Spirits,
                        gets down on all fours
and finds a human woman who will sell to her her shadow:
                        the composer
        said this opera was his "Child of woe,"
                and you yourself staring down
        like the giant ape, surprised to find your hand
                empty, beast to her beauty,
                        are swaying, falling
                through skyscraper horizons
                        to a woman's voice
        singing you to sleep half a century ago
where you're floating downstream among bulrushes and cattails
                toward your rendezvous with Pharaoh's
                        daughter who fades
        into the Domino Sugar Factory's glow
                        as sun
                tangled in bridge cables
        portions out currents quarreling into zones
                        blazing up like gas flames
on the little gas stove in your walkup on First Avenue
above the Ukrainian beauty parlor where you first felt
the world getting down on all fours and you followed along
                in your dog's instinct for pleasure—

it seemed like it would last
forever, didn't it, her reading out from the paper
                    and the two of you laughing together
                            until you both
        lost your shadows and were condemned to walk
among the spirits who cry out to you like cats wawling
            in the weed-clumped frozen garden down below.

Now, the Empress and Emperor sing their final duet
                    in praise of the unborn, drowning out
                        the cats as the river
                            brims over,
                reflecting the schooner Tiger
        shooting flames from topmast to bowsprit,
                    the hull listing,
            sinking into it's own smoking
                hiss and onrush
                    of waters
            buried under fill buried under
                the fallen towers
never dreamed of by the Empress or Emperor
            who sing not to vaporized wisps
                    of DNA
but to spirits crowding into starry vestibules.

And there you are with your crew, wintering over
            as you build the Restless
        and in the first spring wind launch her through
            Hell Gate into the great bay
                beyond, sailing up
            as far as the River of Red Hills
before crossing the wide ocean to your house in Old Wall Street
        you and your wife called The Two Hooded Crows

and where you lie down in your bed
alone because she died while you were at sea, and you only
found out the moment you came ashore—
and that first night
after twenty-five years together, you dream
of furred beasts slinking
through your campsite,
your human smell fading into musk and scat.

Self-Portrait with Shoulder Pads

Brother fighting brother and the loser
driven out, my eyes were on Tim's eyes off some place,

gone from his body, while under his jersey
the shoulder pads gleam brighter,

masculine yoke we both labor under
determined not to get knocked flat—

smashing and smashing into each other, helmets
blankly ringing to the whole team screaming

in time to the drill *Timmy hit Tommy Tommy hit Timmy*
until exhausted we fall to our knees

and still Coach refuses to blow the whistle so that we,
on our knees, keep ramming into each other,

implacable, servile, our hearts too violent
not to play inside the rules.

How we envied the hippies on the *Joe Pyne Show,*
Pyne sneering to Frank Zappa,

"So I guess your long hair makes you a woman,"
Zappa shooting back, "I guess your wooden leg makes you a table."

White as calcium, white as moons brought down
into swampwater, white as a cataract

on a blind eye, the pads fuse onto shoulder bones
to make us walk that athletic walk of power

and glory and terror of shame so Tommy
hitting Timmy and Timmy hitting Tommy

takes over mind and body in the Zone
until Coach blows the whistle and we get up

off our knees and turn to avoid each others' faces.
Years later, brought down by gunflash insights

of assassination and business frowns
of gangbangers dividing up junk

while police held the line in riot masks
and shields, I prayed for the cup to pass.

But either way, I was an ass and had to carry
my ass's load as far as an ass could.

For Benny Andrews

Flannery O'Connor was to us, the African-Americans of her time,
"a white lady." . . . Whenever we'd meet her kind on the streets . . .
racial customs demanded that we step aside . . .
—Benny Andrews, *Race Relations*

So much depends on what you have an ear for.
—Flannery O'Connor

Everything that rises must converge—
but of everything that falls, where does it fall to?
and though we hold the dead as closely as we can
how far, how wide of where we living are . . .
Benny, have you gone back down to your otherworldly
Madison slippery on a mudslick of red clay,
sweet potato sandwiches in your lunch sack?
Chimney-walled shacks, raw pine boards oozing sap,
little muck-holes gouged by hooves out in the yard,
the galvanized roofs all trembly in the rain.
The people you loved to paint, hands big and gangly,
long pointy feet, bodies sway-backed and tall
as if floating on a pool; and those bony, long-eared,
knobby-legged mules, shovel heads thrusting
at the viewer, resigned in their leather blinders
to working out the day for "them white ladies"
you'd have to step aside for—that "artificial
white made world . . ."

            I sense your cross-grained hands
reaching out to mine, your Manhattanized
vernacular slyly joking in my ear,
stretching *"I"* out into a lazy, nasal *"aw"*:
"I'm in the game, Tom, I'm still in the game."
And then the words you once quoted come back

like a refrain, words the white lady wrote
and that you loved in spite of that:
"So much depends on what you have an ear for"—
And then your voice again, admonishing, encouraging,
a phantom drawling in my ear, consoling,
unconsoling, there, not there:

"Gads man, don't you get distracted. You know
how a bird just sits there on its nest,
it doesn't look like much to anyone around,
but it's doing something. And then the egg hatches.
So like I say, do your work, don't get distracted."
And there you are in the studio among heaped up
scraps and rags, your ear for what's abandoned,
thrown out, ignored, become the element
you live in, making it rise again, shine—
though still showing the tatters, the hurt,
the stitches of want nobody can mend, pain
flattened into paint, shreds pinned to canvas
until the urge to rise meets the urge to fall.

Orders of Daylight

1/ Windowpane

The windowpane stippled all over with fine mist
Was a maze the December sun got lost in,
Its rays fractioned, split, then wriggling headfirst
Like sperm for the pulsing lucent ovum.

And all down the street head-bent umbrellas out pacing
Gingko-plastered sidewalks seemed survivors
Intent with getting on with it, outfacing
Bad dreams and balky nerves, the orders

Of daylight taking precedent. As if whatever
Amnesty is yours is only yours by letting go.
As if regret gave off a gleam like the shaved head of a prisoner.
As if death (or what feels like it) were transparent, a window,

A way of looking through yourself into the heart of day:
And who's there to meet your eyes but the guy
In his refrigerator box hanging his socks to dry
On a chainlink clothesline, each drop hugging its own translucency.

2/ Good-bye to All That

When you floundered out into your own no-man's land
It was like the Christmas truce being played out
Between the lines, both sides going beyond
The limits of their uniforms, discipline a rout

As they shared a smoke and traded whiskey
For Schnapps, the officers helpless and relieved
To shrug off for a moment their own authority,
The war given over, promiscuously dissolved.

To be the rabbit that they flushed and killed
Together, to feel the sky unlidded roll
Back to sunned-on fields—if only you could yield
To it, get drunk with it, credit it as real:

And whoever goes free, let them too go past the sentry
Who waves you off the road to a floodbank,
A thawing ditch, and a mockingbird that calls all day
And all night too, oblivious to your station and rank.

3/ Survivor

And say you were the rat down among the subway sleepers
Rearing up on your hind legs, not so much to sniff
The oil fug as to cross over tacit borders
Between yourself and the platform watchers, transgressive

Without knowing it, nose hurrying you on until one foot
Lifts, tensing, sensing a vibration? And now the train
Through miles and miles of rails makes your heart
Pound at its coming—and some synapse fire of vision

Brings back the lost city sinking down under the water
And you swimming among the drowning, swept beyond
Yourself into a tidal river—and you're cast away there,
A stranger outside the tribe, no promised land

To turn to, just your teeth, your always gnawing hunger:
And generations passing, you migrate down
Under the earth, willful, a long term survivor:
And there you are, foraging through trash under the speeding train.

4/ Buoyancy

A swimmer swims out through voids of drypoint, inkwash,
He dives deeper than the artist etching him on the plate
Can follow, he dissolves into blues and blacks, into the hush
Of stone that underlies the waters. And he senses how his fate

Is neither his nor his maker's: who is he that the waters
Should compass him about? Out of synch, in synch,
At the bottom of the sea he finds out his own nature:
Ragged sail; a skim of oil; torn envelopes; a house key blank.

So my swimmer, come back out of the depths,
Remind me how each summer the bottom gives way
To another bottom and another, another . . . that whoever keeps
Going down goes down atmosphere by atmosphere, living it day

By day until the whole ocean's bulk balances on
Your shoulders. And now that you've grown
Up and into it, no one but you can question
This buoyancy that weighs you down.

5/ Shrine

Shadow of a wing across the curtain.
The winter trees so bare the wood rings with light.
And sun keeps falling through plastic bags torn
To streamers in the branches and quiet

Multiplies long hours into the afternoon
And the paperweight with the brain afloat in clear glass
Gives back the slash and criss-cross of my workaday shrine:
A plastic baggie full of my father's ashes;

Three teeth pulled, blood dried on the roots; a hospital bracelet;
A vial of sand from the Sahara; a blown glass dolphin
Arcing across the sea from here back to Murano; and a geode split
In two, amethyst and space rock, bookends of the moon.

How long it takes a life to find its proper altitude:
And here it is, in front of you, emblem and inconsequence,
Concentrated into the paperweight's glass void,
There beside me, beyond me, afloat in pure transparence.

Recording

The first word God said made everything
out of nothing. But the nothing shows through—

through his breathing on the tape cassette,
so slow, so tentatively regular, so almost

at an end although it doesn't end but keeps
refreshing itself over in the quiet

it's recorded in, that it almost seems to float
in like a medium of water, deep down

near the bottom of something too dark
to see through. God isn't speaking to him breathing

in his coma breath, God is saying nothing
inside the nothing out of which the everything

is waiting for his breath to breathe into it.
My friend's breath is running out. Only on this tape

can I hear him as he lies there. His breathing
is the breath that makes me catch my own breath

coming into my lungs as the sound comes
into my ears and into my brain and into some where

inside me I know is being hollowed out
by each breath of his preparing a nothing

that is so dark and seamless I lose sight
of him being borne away on the currents

of his breathing that inflates into the everything
the nothing wants to be. When he lay there,

shrinking back away from sunset, the nurse said
his fear was common, called "sundowning."

And when he finally settled down, and later sank
into a coma, he began breathing just this way,

breath flowing out, flowing in, while the nothing
moved on the face of everything and God

climbed down into the rising of it.

Song That Can Only Be Sung Once

after Porfirio Barba Jacob's Cancion De La Vida Profunda

Variable, changeable, yes, there are days when
people like us are like that. Maybe under

some other sky something like glory smiles on us,
maybe there life is clear, maybe there things open up

on the way the sea stretches out to the horizon—
but us, we're blown by chance the way wind blows

blades of grass lightly blowing them all one way.

And then there are days when we feel April,
the fields of April making us feel our bodies

longing to be held and fucked into oblivion,
bodies fertile as a field in April, swollen,

trembling to be touched: and under the influences
of rains pouring down as if pure spirit poured

into us like rain, that thing called "soul"
sprouts and branches and entangles us

in lush bowers and thickets of illusion.

Oh yes, days come along when we're calm, clear
—childhood sunsets, lagoons rippling sapphire!—

days when a verse, a sudden whistle, days when a mountain
and bird passing over it, days when even our own pain

and what we feel it to be like make us smile.

And sure, there are days when we're so
disgusting, so sordid to ourselves

it's like we're dark stone in the darkness
inside flint: then nighttime surprises us,

its lamplight dizzying, cold, profuse, glinting
off tossed coins of the good, the terrible

shining with the gleam of that primal metal.

And other days come, come when women
want to cry their come cries and use us

as their own, days when we're itching to get
a woman naked, and then we can't face it, can't

stand it somehow, they want us but we don't know
how to want them back: arm tightening around

a waist, hand cupping a breast, we don't dare
touch the roundness of an apple or a pear,

the round earth spins us off into space.

And then there arrive days so dismal and stupefied
and numb that the idiot soughing of a pine grove

sounds like weeping: and what some idiot called
the soul whines and wails and carries on

with what some other idiot calls "the pain of the world":
and maybe not God himself, that absolute fool,

can make that wind less cutting, or make it stop.

And then there comes, certain to come, oh my earth
I love beyond any of my days, a day . . . a day . . . a day

when my sail catches the wind and drags the anchor
up out of the bottom muck, and nothing can withstand

that wind blowing by, talking to itself, talking, talking . . .
and the day is mine and yours and every living thing's . . .

the day when nobody and nothing can keep us
from getting up and going, no matter who we are . . .

the day when our leaving is the same as our arriving.

Mingus Reborn as Mingus

So—Mingus tells Mingus, *Hold your breath, hold the next one,*
keep on holding it till you sink down to death . . .
And who should Mingus see but Fats coughing blood,
dead at 23, Bird without wings, but no G-O-D—

no Jesus, neither, just Fat's trumpet changing the wind's velocity
as a man like my man comes walking through vapor
streaming from stagelights—and so Mingus slips back
into the man's skin and feels the old pimp hat's

too tight brim as he picks up the bass and stares
stranded from the bandstand at the crowd's hungry,
knife and fork face—and so dead meat Mingus enters
the soul of sinner Mingus, tormented pimp Mingus,

beneath the underdog St. Mingus of the old cold facts
who bows his bass like a demon in his hands, playing
"Hellview of Bellevue" with a look on his face
that says, I don't *really* want to die, but I am.

NOTES

General Note

During the summer of 2007, I was in Lebanon doing some journalism about the aftermath of the 2006 Israeli-Lebanese War, and Lebanon was still digging out from under the rubble. While I was there, the worst internal civil conflict since the 1975–1990 Lebanese Civil War broke out in Beirut and other parts of the country, such as Tripoli, where a Palestinian refugee camp, Nahr al-Bahred, was totally destroyed. The violence would culminate in May 2008, when armed clashes broke out between rival Beirut political factions. However obliquely, several poems respond to these events.

"Army Cats"

CP stands for Command Post.

Bast, also known as Lady of Flame and Eye of Ra, is an ancient Egyptian cat goddess.

I came across the detail about the cats being nailed to shields in Tom Holland's *Persian Fire*.

"Beirut Tank"

The Corniche is Beirut's seafront promenade where many people gather to look at the Pigeon Rocks, two giant limestone natural arch formations that jut several hundred feet up out of the sea.

The curses aren't meant to be exact transliterations, though certainly Arabic equivalents exist.

"Stranding"

Captain MacMorris is an Irish soldier fighting for the English in Shakespeare's *Henry V.*

"For the Executive Director of the Fallen"

The poem is in memory of Liam Rector. The ending is loosely based on the Noh play, "Sumida-gawa River."

"Revenant"

See Note on "Beirut Tank" for the Pigeon Rocks.

"Pig from Ohio"

The 16 acre, 70 foot hole is the site of the former World Trade Towers.

"A Wedding at Cana, Lebanon, 2007"

Fairouz is a Lebanese diva famous throughout the Arab world.

"This Thing of Darkness"

The title is a quote from Shakespeare's *The Tempest,* in which Prospero says of Caliban: ". . . this thing of darkness I / Acknowledge mine."

"A Promise"

Some of the lines are adapted from Primo Levi's *Is This a Man?* and *Moments of Reprieve.*

"The Games"

Sections "2/ At the Party," "3/ The Sack": In Etruscan tomb painting, the god of death, Charun, holds a hammer as he leads the dead to the other world.

Section "4/ A Citizen of the Empire": Meat from slaughtered beasts was often passed out to Rome's citizenry.

Section "5/ Portents": Constantine's gigantic marble foot is in the Capitoline Museum. The portents were taken from Tom Holland's *Crossing the Rubicon*. And the story of the Arimaspian's and the griffins occurs in Herodotus's *Histories*.

"Spell"

The spell is based on a spell taken from the *Greek Magical Papyri*, translated by Hans Dieter Betz.

"On First Avenue and Sixth Street"

The opera referred to is the Richard Strauss/Hugo von Hoffmaanstahl collaboration, *Die Frau Ohne Schatten*.

Some of the remains of the *Tyger* are buried under the former World Trade Towers site.

"Orders of Daylight"

Section "2/ *Good-bye to All That*": The title of section 2 is taken from Robert Graves's World War I memoir of the same name. The Christmas Truce refers to the spontaneous fraternization in No Man's Land during World War I between British and German troops on Christmas Eve, 1914, along the Western Front.

"Recording"

The first line is adapted from a statement by Paul Valéry.

"Mingus Reborn as Mingus"

Charles Mingus wrote an autobiography called *Beneath the Underdog*. One of his compositions is called "Hellview of Bellevue."

Acknowledgments

The author would like to thank the Kingsley Tufts Award of the Claremont Graduate University for its support, as well as the following publications in which many of these poems were first published:

Agenda: "Shrine"

Agni: "A Promise," "For Benny Andrews"

The American Poetry Review: "After a Rembrandt Motif," "Fenix," "On First Avenue and Sixth Street," "Orders of Daylight," "Self-Portrait with Shoulder Pads," "To Death"

The Atlantic Monthly: "Buoyancy"

The Cortland Review: "O. D."

Dossier: "Revenant," "Spell," "Money"

Harvard Review: "Speech for a Fly," "Mingus Reborn as Mingus"

The New Yorker: "Army Cats," "Hunter Gatherer"

Ploughshares: "Pig from Ohio," "The Chosen One," "Round"

Poetry: "Beirut Tank," "Stranding," "For the Executive Director of the Fallen," "Song That Can Only Be Sung Once"

Poetry London: "On First Avenue and Sixth Street"

Slate: "Wedding at Cana, Lebanon, 2007," "Recording"

The Threepenny Review: "Triumph"

The Virginia Quarterly Review: "Border Crossings," "Refugee"

Anthologies:

Poems about Space, Gulbenkian Foundation: "For a Spacesuit Set Adrift"

Shakespeare Year Book: "This Thing of Darkness"

This book is for Sarah, Alan, Michael, and Robert for their help and encouragement, and Ellen, for her friendship.

TOM SLEIGH is the author of eight collections of poetry, including *Space Walk*, winner of the Kingsley Tufts Poetry Award, and *Far Side of the Earth;* a collection of essays, *Interview with a Ghost;* and a translation of Euripides' *Herakles*. He has won the Shelley Prize from the Poetry Society of America, an Academy of Arts and Letters Award in Literature, and grants and awards from the Guggenheim Foundation, the National Endowment for the Arts, and the Lila Wallace Fund. He is a Distinguished Professor at Hunter College, where he teaches in the MFA Program, and he lives in Brooklyn, New York.

Book design by Rachel Holscher. Composition by
BookMobile Design and Publishing Services, Minneapolis, Minnesota.
Manufactured by Versa Press on acid-free
30 percent postconsumer wastepaper.